Jurassic Profit

Jurassic Profit

Matthew Petchinsky

1

Jurassic Profit: Unearth Your Inner Millionaire Fossil

By: Matthew Petchinsky

Disclaimer

Important Notice:

Jurassic Profit: Unearth Your Inner Millionaire Fossil is a creative personal-development and financial-motivation guide. The concepts, metaphors, and frameworks presented throughout this book—including fossil-based analogies, prehistoric metaphors, evolution-inspired strategies, and imaginative comparisons—are **symbolic tools designed for mindset transformation**. They are **not literal instructions**, nor do they represent scientific claims, paleontological facts, or guaranteed financial outcomes.

This book does **not** provide financial, legal, accounting, tax, investment, or professional business advice. While strategies, reflections, and examples within this text may offer educational insights or perspective shifts, they are **generalized in nature** and may not apply to every individual's personal, financial, or business circumstances.

Readers should always consult with a licensed financial advisor, attorney, accountant, or certified professional before making any financial decisions, investments, or changes related to their personal or business strategy.

All exercises, wealth-building suggestions, and mindset techniques described in this book are voluntary and should be used at the reader's discretion. The author makes **no promises of earnings**, no guarantees of specific results, and no assurances that following any information in this book will lead to monetary gain, business success, or increased income.

Past performance does not guarantee future results. Any examples of financial success mentioned in this book are **illustrative only** and should not be interpreted as typical, expected, or promised outcomes.

This book incorporates imaginative, metaphor-driven, and prehistoric-themed language intended solely for creative engagement. References to dinosaurs, fossils, excavation, ancient biology, or evolutionary concepts are **creative devices**, not factual predictions or scientific instruction.

This book does **not** claim affiliation with, authorization from, or endorsement by any paleontological institution, scientific organization, or intellectual property related to the Jurassic franchise or any other media entity.

By reading this book, the reader acknowledges that they are solely responsible for their own decisions, actions, financial choices, and outcomes. The author and publisher assume **no responsibility or liability** for any losses, damages, or consequences arising from the application or misinterpretation of the information provided.

If you are experiencing financial hardship, legal issues, business instability, or psychological stress related to money, please seek assistance from qualified professionals or mental-health providers.

This book is offered in the spirit of empowerment, creativity, and inspiration. Its purpose is to help readers explore new perspectives, ignite inner potential, and think boldly about their financial future—while understanding that **true success depends on individual effort, timing, market conditions, and personal responsibility.**

By continuing to read, you agree to these terms.

Introduction

You are standing on buried treasure—ancestral skills, instincts, and insights encoded in your evolutionary bones. Let's excavate.

Every generation searches for a blueprint to wealth, but what if the map isn't in a spreadsheet, a seminar, or a guru's podcast? What if the real secrets of building a modern empire are buried not in the ground—but inside **you**?

Long before skyscrapers, stock markets, or digital economies, our ancestors survived and thrived using instincts that were precise, adaptive, and unstoppable. They were hunters, gatherers, strategists, observers, builders, and problem-solvers. They negotiated with nature, competed with predators, and read landscapes the way you scroll a screen. Their wealth was survival. Their currency was awareness. Their success was the ability to transform chaos into opportunity.

Those instincts didn't disappear.

They fossilized.

Inside every person lies an **inner millionaire fossil**—a set of dormant strengths shaped by evolution, waiting to be exhumed and put to work. But like any buried treasure, it takes intention, curiosity, and the right tools to dig it out. That is what this book is: a field guide, a pickaxe, and a lamp illuminating the forgotten chambers of your potential.

What if your next million isn't something you create from scratch—but something you uncover?

In today's world of overcomplication—algorithms, trends, market noise—we forget the primal principles that built the earliest human empires. This book helps you return to them. Through quirky stories, prehistoric metaphors, fossil-based frameworks, and evolution-inspired exercises, **Jurassic Profit** teaches you how to spot opportunities like a raptor, adapt like an early mammal, guard your empire like a titan of the ancient world, and build wealth using the same instincts that kept your ancestors alive.

Each chapter is an excavation site.
A layer of insight.
A reveal of something you already possess.

You will learn to:

- **Unearth your hidden financial instincts**
- **Recognize your natural strengths as evolutionary assets**
- **Sharpen ancient decision-making tools for modern business**
- **Transform dormant potential into scalable wealth**
- **Build your empire with the resilience of creatures that survived millions of years**

This isn't about hustling harder.
This is about **remembering who you are**.

The old world left clues. Fossils. Patterns. Lessons etched in bone. Your success isn't built on something new—it's built on something timeless.

Brush away the dust.
The excavation begins now.
Your million-year-old millionaire is waiting to emerge.

Chapter One – Bone Mining Your Value

You are standing on buried treasure—vast, ancient, practical wealth potential fossilized inside your instincts. Chapter One is your excavation site, where we dig beneath fear, doubt, and modern overwhelm to uncover the primal intelligence that once determined survival. That same intelligence now determines your financial rise.

Modern wealth-building is not about reinventing yourself. It's about **remembering** yourself.

It's about chiseling away the hardened layers of conditioning until the true structure of your value—your "profit skeleton"—emerges.

Your ancestors survived because they were watchers, trackers, strategists, builders, and adaptors. Those skills didn't vanish. They fossilized into you. And now you will dig them up, polish them, and use them as tools for empire-building.

Excavation Begins — What Is "Bone Mining"?

Bone Mining is the art of digging beneath the noise of modern life to uncover the *core traits* that make you naturally capable of earning more.

Bone Mining asks:

- What am I naturally built to do?
- What instincts do I ignore?
- What skills do I take for granted?
- What value have I buried under guilt, fear, or insecurity?
- What behavior patterns hint at untapped earning power?

Your bones—your structure—tell your story.

They're the blueprint for your wealth behavior.

Just like paleontologists uncover life forms from dust, you will uncover your forgotten financial instincts from the layers of your daily habits and personality.

The Fossil Layers of Hidden Wealth

Hidden financial instincts manifest in subtle ways:

1. Pattern Recognition

You see trends weeks or months before others realize something is shifting.
This is a survival instinct—spotting changes in the environment.

2. Resource Awareness

You can stretch resources or reallocate them instinctively.
This is ancestral frugality turned into modern optimization.

3. Gut Logic

Your intuition fires before your thoughts do.
This is the "quiet predator sense" that saved your ancestors from threats.

4. Adaptation Reflex

You improvise quickly, shift strategies with ease.
That's evolution acting through you.

5. Opportunity Scavenging

You notice leftover, unused, rejected opportunities others overlook.
This is the scavenger instinct—one of the most profitable in nature.

6. Energy Management

You can push, rest, and pace yourself instinctively.
This is ancient survival pacing—now crucial to business endurance.

These instincts aren't new.
They're simply buried.

Your wealth journey begins by dusting them off.

12 Profitable Ways to Monetize Your Primal Value

Below are **twelve fossil-grade income streams** directly tied to your instincts. These aren't theoretical—they're practical, scalable, and instinct-approved.

1. Creating Books (Your Infinite Asset Factory)

Books are modern fossils—permanent, replicable, and scalable. You can produce them fast, sell them worldwide, and build an empire without gatekeepers.

2. Digital Courses

Teach what you know. Record once, earn forever.

3. Freelancing Your Natural Skillset

Writing, designing, researching, or organizing—your instincts reveal what you can monetize today.

4. Print-On-Demand Products

Merch, journals, planners, ritual books, and themed collections based on your niche.

5. Affiliate Marketing

Recommending products you already love—no inventory needed.

6. AI-Assisted Services

Prompts, templates, story rewriting, outline creation—skills almost everyone needs.

7. YouTube or TikTok Content

Short educational or entertaining videos that compound views over time.

8. Niche Expertise Coaching

Everyone has a niche. Everyone has a beginner behind them who needs guidance.

9. Skill Licensing

Templates, frameworks, and unique ideas can be licensed to others.

10. Newsletter or Membership

Curate insights regularly; charge monthly for access to your mind.

11. Consulting or Problem-Solving Services

Businesses pay heavily for clarity, strategy, and solutions.

12. Digital Asset Creation

Ebooks, workbooks, audio guides, tools, planners—anything downloadable is infinite.

These 12 income streams are the bones of modern wealth creation. Pick 1–3 to start. Your instincts will point you toward the right ones.

Fossil Clues — Signs You Underestimate Yourself

If you experience any of these, your financial instincts are buried:

- You downplay skills others praise.
- You hesitate to charge money.
- You think your abilities are "nothing special."
- You compare yourself to others instead of studying yourself.
- You wait for permission to begin.

These are not signs of weakness.
These are signs of **unmined value**.

Your inner millionaire fossil is there.
You just haven't brushed off the dirt yet.

The Excavation Ritual — Unlocking Your Value
To Bone Mine your value:

1. Identify what you naturally do well.
2. Link that trait to at least one of the 12 wealth streams.
3. Create a simple plan to monetize it.
4. Act quickly, before doubt hardens into stone again.
5. Repeat with new traits weekly.

Your value is not a mystery.
It's a structure waiting to be revealed.

10 Journal Prompts for Chapter One: Bone Mining Your Value

1. What do people naturally come to me for help with?
2. Which instinctive skills feel "easy" to me but "hard" to others?
3. What value have I ignored because it feels too natural or obvious?
4. What behaviors show up when I'm under pressure—and how could they be strengths?
5. What patterns do I notice that others ignore?
6. What fears have buried my talents under "dirt"?
7. Which of the 12 income streams feels most aligned with my instincts?
8. What did I love doing as a child before self-doubt formed?
9. What "fossil" of potential—something old, forgotten, or dormant—still lives in me?
10. If I believed my instincts were sacred and wise, how would I act differently starting today?

Closing Reflection

You have just taken the first step into your excavation. You brushed away the dust and caught your first glimpse of the structure beneath—your value, your instincts, your evolutionary wealth. Nothing you discovered today is new. It has always been inside you, waiting for sunlight.

Your ancestors survived with less knowledge, fewer tools, and far more danger. You carry their resilience in your bones. You carry their brilliance in your instincts. And now, for the first time in years—maybe decades—you've begun to listen to that ancient voice.

You're not building wealth from scratch.

You're **unearthing it**, piece by piece.

Your bones hold the blueprint.

Your instincts hold the instructions.
Your future holds the empire.

Tomorrow, we move from excavation… to construction.
You've found the bones.
Next, we turn them into your business skeleton.

Chapter Two – Fossil-Based Business Plans

A fossil tells a story: what a creature was built for, how it survived, how it hunted, how it moved, and how it dominated its environment. Your business is no different.

Most people build businesses backwards—copying what's trendy, forcing themselves into models that don't match their instincts, and wondering why they burn out. But in the prehistoric world, creatures didn't survive by imitating others. They survived by becoming what **they were built to be**.

This chapter teaches you to craft a business plan that mirrors your evolutionary strengths—the internal architecture you uncovered in Chapter One. Your instincts are your competitive advantage. Your business plan is simply the skeleton that holds them together.

A strong creature has a strong skeleton.
A strong business has a strong structure.
Today, you build yours.

What Is a Fossil-Based Business Plan?

A fossil-based business plan is not a corporate blueprint.
It is a **biological, instinct-driven strategy** built around:

- Your natural strengths
- Your instinctive decision patterns
- Your energetic rhythm
- Your unique value
- Your aligned income streams

Instead of forcing yourself into someone else's business model, you reconstruct a structure that fits *your natural design.*

Think of this chapter as assembling your wealth skeleton.

The Ribcage of Revenue — Your 3 Core Income Streams

Ancient creatures didn't depend on one survival method. Neither should you.

Your three core income streams form the **ribcage**—the protective, stabilizing structure that ensures your business survives economic shifts, setbacks, or slow seasons.

Choose three **aligned** streams from the 12 you explored earlier.

Examples:

- Books + YouTube + Consulting
- Courses + Membership + Templates
- Freelancing + Digital Products + Affiliate Marketing

Your ribcage ensures:

1. Diversification
2. Stability
3. Predictability
4. Scalability

This alignment reduces overwhelm because each stream uses the same bones—your strengths.

The Spine — Your Primal Purpose and Core Message

A spine holds everything upright.
Your business spine answers three ancient questions:

1. What do I want my business to stand for?
(E.g., empowerment, transformation, results, creativity)

2. What does my audience need from me instinctively?
(E.g., clarity, hope, confidence, relief, skills)

3. What is the ONE message my brand carries?
(E.g., "You can rebuild yourself," "Your instincts are your power," etc.)

This spine must be clear, stable, and strong.

Skull & Teeth — Your Brand Identity and Market Bite

The skull protects the brain—your ideas.

The teeth are your bite—your presence in the market.

Your brand becomes unforgettable when:

- Your visuals are consistent
- Your tone is unmistakable
- Your value is sharp and clear
- Your message has "bite"—something bold and primal

Your bite marks are what people remember.

The Legs — How Your Business Moves

Your business doesn't just exist; it must **move**, grow, and hunt opportunity.

Your legs are simply:

- Your daily actions
- Your weekly systems
- Your monthly momentum
- The rhythm you naturally operate in

Instead of fighting your energy, you work with your instincts:

If you're built for speed → rapid creation model
If you're built for endurance → long-term growth model
If you're built for bursts → cyclic creation model
If you're built for precision → high-ticket model

Your bones determine your movement.

The Fossil Reconstruction Business Plan

(Use this as a full guided exercise with real output. This is the core of Chapter 2.)

This exercise builds your entire business plan using your instincts as the blueprint.

STEP 1 — Identify Your Fossil Traits (Your Evolutionary Strengths)

List 5 instincts or strengths from Chapter 1 that define how you operate.

Examples:

- Pattern recognition
- Problem-solving
- Creative speed
- Deep-focus endurance
- Emotional intuition
- Strategic patience

Write yours:

These traits will direct every part of your business plan.

STEP 2 — Choose Your Three Ribcage Revenue Streams

Pick 3 aligned income methods from the 12 presented earlier.

Ask yourself: *Which of these uses my instincts the most naturally?*

STEP 3 — Define Your Business Spine (Purpose + Message)
Answer the following:

1. My business exists to:
(Empower, teach, heal, inspire, simplify, etc.)

2. My audience is craving:
(Ease, confidence, structure, hope, direction, strategy)

3. My core message—the idea my brand stands on—is:
This becomes the backbone of your empire.

STEP 4 — Build Your Skull & Teeth (Brand Identity)
Answer:

What is the personality of my brand?
(Fierce, ancient, wise, primal, modern, inspiring, sharp)

What colors or visuals feel instinctively right for my brand?

What makes my message have bite?
(E.g., bold claims, primal metaphors, transformation)

Your skull protects your ideas.
Your teeth leave a mark.

STEP 5 — Shape Your Legs (Movement System)
Answer:

How do I naturally get things done?
(Fast bursts? One-hour sprints? Long sessions? Daily flow?)

What is my ideal weekly rhythm for content/work?

What small daily actions move my business forward?

Your movement system = momentum.

STEP 6 — Assemble Your Skeleton
Put it all together:

- Instincts = bones
- Core income streams = ribcage
- Brand message = spine
- Brand identity = skull
- Movement system = legs

You now have a **living, breathing business organism** built around who you are.

This is your **Fossil-Based Business Plan**.

Why This Method Works

Most business plans fail because they are built on:

- force instead of instinct
- imitation instead of originality
- pressure instead of alignment
- confusion instead of clarity

Your fossil plan is the opposite.
It's structural, primal, and permanent.

You're not building a business like everyone else.
You're building one designed by evolution itself.

10 Journal Prompts for Chapter Two: Fossil-Based Business Plans

1. What instincts from Chapter One feel strongest today?
2. Which three income streams feel the most natural and energizing?
3. What problem am I instinctively built to solve?
4. What message do I wish someone told *me* years ago?
5. How would my business look if it perfectly matched my personality?
6. What brand identity feels like "home"—not forced?
7. What is my natural working rhythm, and how can I honor it?
8. What fears arise when I imagine building a bigger business structure?
9. What strengths have I undervalued in myself that belong in my plan?
10. What part of my fossil-based plan feels the most exciting to start today?

Closing Reflection for Chapter Two

Your business now has bones.
A structure.
A skeleton powerful enough to support your dreams.

You didn't build this plan by copying someone else.
You built it by digging into the deepest, most ancient parts of yourself—your instincts, your strengths, your energy, your nature. Everything about this plan is **yours**. It fits you. It breathes you. It moves like you move.

Most people never do this work.
They build fragile systems with no spine, no bite, no identity, no instinctual support.
Their businesses collapse because they were never created to survive.

But yours is different.
Yours is an organism built from million-year-old logic and modern ambition.
It's not another business—it's a living structure made from your bones and potential.

You have unearthed your value.
You have built your skeleton.
Next, in Chapter Three, you learn how to protect it—how to escape the financial tar pits that trap millions of people.

The excavation continues.
Your empire is forming.

Chapter Three – Tar Pits of Debt and How to Escape

In the prehistoric world, tar pits weren't just sticky pools in the earth—they were **silent death traps**. Creatures didn't fall in because they were weak. They fell in because the tar looked safe. It looked solid. It looked like something they could step on and use to move forward.

Debt operates the same way.

It offers the illusion of stability—help in the moment, relief today—but beneath the surface lies a thick, pulling force that slowly consumes financial potential, energy, and momentum. What begins as a single step becomes a sinkhole. The more you panic and thrash, the deeper you go.

To escape, you don't fight harder.

You **think smarter**.

You behave strategically.

You activate the evolutionary decision-making tools your ancestors used when survival was on the line.

This chapter teaches you:

- How debt functions like a tar pit
- Why panic is the real enemy
- How your instincts can help you escape
- How to break free using ancient logic and modern strategy
- How to rebuild your movement once you're free

Debt isn't a moral failure.

It is a **trap**—and every trap has an escape sequence.

Today, you learn yours.

Understanding the Tar Pit Mindset

Creatures fell into tar pits for three main reasons:

1. Misjudgment

They thought the ground was stable.
Debt often begins with the same misjudgment—"I can handle this," "I'll pay it off soon," "This isn't so deep."

2. Hunger

The promise of an easy meal lured them in.
Debt offers easy rewards: instant gratification, immediate relief, fast solutions.

3. Panic Response

Once stuck, they struggled violently.
In finances, panic results in:

- Ignoring mail
- Avoiding statements
- Letting balances grow
- Avoiding responsibility

Panic accelerates sinking.
Stillness begins the escape.

Debt isn't about bad choices, laziness, or failure.
Debt is about **instincts misfiring in a modern environment**.

Your goal is not blame.
Your goal is understanding—and then liberation.

Ancient Decision-Making — The Survival Logic You Need

Your ancestors survived because they made decisions based on:

1. Environmental Assessment

Before moving, they scanned the landscape.

2. Slow Initial Movement

They approached unknown terrain with caution.

3. Pattern-Based Recognition

Small signals meant danger.

4. Strategic Action, Not Emotional Reaction

Emotion killed.
Strategy saved.

Apply these principles to debt and you immediately stop sinking.

The Tar Pit Mechanics — Why Debt Grabs You

Debt pulls you in because of:

1. Interest Creep

Like tar thickening around legs, interest compounds quietly. Most people underestimate its power.

2. Emotional Weight

Debt creates shame, fear, and avoidance—exactly what keeps people from escaping.

3. Psychological Freeze

Avoidance slows decision-making until nothing happens and balances balloon.

4. Time Elongation

Like a creature sinking slowly, debt traps you month after month, one inch at a time.

But here's the truth:

The deeper you think you are, the more reachable the escape actually is.

The tar pit has edges.
And you can get out.

The Escape Strategy — Your Instinctual Debt Freedom Blueprint

To survive the tar pit, ancient creatures needed four things:

1. **Stillness**
2. **Assessment**
3. **A strategic plan**
4. **A slow, precise escape**

Your financial escape mirrors these exact steps.

STEP 1: STILLNESS — Stop Thrashing

Panic increases your financial quicksand.
Stopping thrashing means:

- No new debt
- No emotional spending
- No avoidance
- No guessing
- No denial

Your first victory is awareness without action.

STEP 2: ASSESSMENT — Map the Tar Pit
List everything:

- Total debt
- Interest rates
- Minimum payments
- Emotional triggers
- Spending patterns
- Which debts feel "sticky"
- Which ones you fear the most

This isn't self-judgment.
This is **environmental scanning**.
Once mapped, the tar pit becomes visible.

STEP 3: STRATEGY — Pick Your Escape Path

You have 3 instinct-driven pathways:

Path A: The Raptor Attack (Aggressive First Strike)

Target the highest-interest debt first.
Use bursts of effort—the instinct of rapid hunters.

Path B: The Sauropod Method (Massive Consistency)

Pick the smallest debt and crush it.
Use momentum—the instinct of steady giants.

Path C: The Burrower Strategy (Invisible Growth)

Cut expenses quietly and drastically redirect money.
Minimal movement, maximum impact.

Choose the path that aligns with your nature.
Evolution wants you to fight with your strengths.

STEP 4: PRECISION MOVEMENT — The Monthly Escape Cycle

Each month:

1. Pay minimums on all debts
2. Attack one debt with every spare dollar
3. Reduce 1–2 expenses
4. Track progress weekly
5. Celebrate every small shift (momentum matters)

No panic.
No rushing.
Just strategic movement.

Strength After Escape — Rebuilding Your Financial Muscles

Once you escape a tar pit, your muscles are weak.
Your confidence is low.
Your energy is drained.

This is natural.

So you rebuild slowly with:

1. A simple emergency buffer

Even \$20–\$50 a month strengthens your survival sense.

2. A spending ritual

Ask: "Is this sinking or supporting?"

3. A re-mapping session every 30 days

Assess and adapt, just like migrating creatures.

4. A small wealth-building action weekly

Books, digital assets, videos, products—your instincts will tell you where to start.

You escaped the pit.
Now you build your path forward.

The Psychological Shift — You're Not a Creature Being Consumed. You're One Evolving.

Debt convinces you:

- You're stuck
- You're helpless
- You're too late
- You've ruined things

But this is a lie.

Evolution doesn't punish the trapped.
It rewards the ones who **learn**, **adapt**, and **move strategically**.

You are not sinking.
You are emerging.
You are evolving.
You are reclaiming terrain.

10 Journal Prompts for Chapter Three: Tar Pits of Debt and How to Escape

1. What emotions surface when I think about my debt?
2. Which part of the tar pit analogy resonates with my experience the most?
3. What would my ancestors do if they faced something like debt?
4. Where do I panic in my financial decision-making?
5. What does my "stillness" step look like in real life?
6. Which escape path (Raptor, Sauropod, Burrower) aligns with my nature?
7. What single habit led me deepest into the tar pit?
8. What single habit will lead me out?
9. What would freedom from debt *feel* like in my body?
10. What is the first small movement I can make today to escape?

Closing Reflection

Debt tries to convince you that you are finished, stuck, sinking, and doomed. But today you learned that every trap has an edge—and every creature, even the ones buried to their chest, had a way out if they stopped thrashing and began thinking.

You learned that your instincts are not your enemies—they are your escape tools. The same ancient logic that guided your ancestors away from predators, cliffs, and danger can guide you out of modern financial traps.

You are not helpless.
You are not sinking beyond recovery.
You are not consumed.

You are becoming **aware**, **strategic**, and **powerful**.

Most people never escape their tar pits because they never change their mindset. But you are different. You are the kind of person who studies the terrain, understands the danger, and then climbs out with precision and resilience.

You're no longer in the pit.
You're on the edge now.
And Chapter Four teaches you how to move from survival...
to flow, abundance, and evolutionary wealth psychology.

The escape is complete.

The evolution continues.

Chapter Four – Egg Hoarding vs. Dino Giving: Wealth Flow Psychology

In the prehistoric world, every creature faced a single, defining question:

Do I hoard my resources, or do I share them with my environment?

Some dinosaurs protected their eggs with obsessive vigilance. Others laid dozens at a time, giving freely to chance, nature, and fate. Both instincts served a purpose—one ensured survival through **protection**, the other through **abundance and spread**.

Humans inherited both.

These ancient survival instincts now show up in your financial life as:

- **Egg Hoarding** → fear-based saving, overprotection, withholding effort
- **Dino Giving** → reckless spending, overcommitment, excessive generosity

The modern world calls it:

scarcity mindset vs. abundance mindset,

but the truth is far deeper—it's biological, evolutionary, and patterned in your bones.

This chapter reveals how your ancient resource instincts shape your wealth flow—and how balancing them unlocks scalable, stable, exponential growth.

You cannot build an empire with only fear.

You cannot sustain one with only generosity.

You need the evolutionary balance between the two.

Today, you learn that balance.

The Two Ancient Money Instincts

Your wealth psychology contains two opposing but necessary forces:

1. The Egg Hoarder

This instinct hoards resources because:

- Loss feels dangerous
- The future feels unpredictable
- Control equals safety
- Scarcity feels familiar

Signs you are Egg Hoarding today:

- You cling to money even when investing is safe
- You feel guilt when spending on yourself
- You fear risk even when the reward is high
- You "wait for the perfect moment"
- You don't share your gifts, skills, or opportunities

Egg Hoarding creates emotional safety…
but financial stagnation.

2. The Dino Giver
This instinct gives, spends, and shares because:

- Community was once survival
- Movement equals opportunity
- Generosity builds alliances
- Spread increases chances of success

Signs you are Dino Giving today:

- You overspend
- You invest impulsively
- You give away your time or skills too freely
- You financially rescue others
- You buy "hope" instead of tools

Dino Giving creates flow...
but without boundaries, it drains your empire.

The Paradox — Both Instincts Are Ancient AND Necessary
Humans evolved with both survival models:

- The Egg Hoarder protects the nest
- The Dino Giver expands the terrain

But wealth requires the **third path**—the evolutionary balance:

Strategic Flow
= A system where money, energy, and resources move with purpose instead of fear or impulse.

This chapter teaches you to create that system.

The Fossil Psychology of Money Flow

Wealth is not built by hoarding or leaking.
It is built by **circulation with intention**.

Your ancestors circulated resources through:

- Trading
- Shelter building
- Tribe cooperation
- Shared hunts
- Redistribution for survival

This instinct is still alive in you.
But modern money requires strategy to channel it effectively.

Today you learn the three wealth-flow models:

Model 1 – The Stagnant Nest (Too Much Hoarding)

This happens when wealth comes in... and never moves. The result:

- No growth
- No investments
- No expansion
- Stress increases because money feels scarce

This is financial **extinction behavior**.

Model 2 – The Leaking Nest (Too Much Giving)

This happens when wealth moves... but without intention. The result:

- Drained accounts
- Impulsive spending
- Burnout
- Shame cycles

This is financial **energy hemorrhage**.

Model 3 – The Evolving Nest (Balanced Flow)

This happens when wealth moves **with precision**. The result:

- Growth
- Stability
- Protection
- Scalable expansion

This is **Strategic Flow**, the goal of this chapter.

Wealth Flow Archetypes — Which One Are You?

Answer these with honesty:

If you are mostly an Egg Hoarder:

- You need safe expansion
- You need micro-investments
- You need confidence through small moves
- You need a controlled flow system

If you are mostly a Dino Giver:

- You need boundaries
- You need spending awareness
- You need slow decision-making
- You need a pause ritual before using money

If you are both:

Perfect.

You have the natural instincts for wealth scaling.

Now you learn how to shape them.

The Wealth Flow Balancer – Your Evolutionary System
Use this 4-step system to align your instincts with scalable wealth.

STEP 1: Identify Your Default Instinct
Are you a hoarder or a giver?
Write a list of behaviors from the past month:

- What did you spend money on?
- What did you avoid investing in?
- What did you share too freely?
- Where did you freeze?

Your pattern reveals your instinct.

STEP 2: Set Your 50/30/20 Evolution Ratio
This is your money flow skeleton:

- **50% Needs (Foundation)**
- **30% Growth (Investments, tools, books, business building)**
- **20% Desire (Comfort, fun, non-essentials)**

The ratio activates flow *without danger or depletion*.

STEP 3: Create Your Movement Ritual (Your "Money Instinct Pause")
Before spending or hoarding, ask:
"Is this survival, impulse, or evolution?"
This question trains your ancient instincts to respond, not react.

STEP 4: Establish Your Wealth Territory

This consists of:

- A monthly business-building goal
- A weekly income action
- A daily microwealth habit

These actions expand your financial environment the way dinosaurs expanded their territory.

Transforming Dormant Potential Into Scalable Wealth

This is where the magic happens.
You activate wealth by:

- Turning your creativity into digital assets
- Turning your ideas into books
- Turning your skills into services
- Turning your instincts into decisions
- Turning your energy into systems

Dormant potential is simply **untouched wealth**.
When you balance hoarding and giving, your potential becomes:

- Renewable
- Scalable
- Stable
- Predictable
- Abundant

You become a creature of **flow**, not fear.

The Evolution Ritual — Daily Wealth Flow Practice
Use this ritual daily:

1. **Sit still and observe your "egg" (your money).**
2. **Identify your instinctive urge (hoard or give).**
3. **Ask the Money Instinct Pause Question.**
4. **Redirect the instinct into evolution.**

Examples:

- Hoarding? → Invest $5 in yourself.
- Giving? → Pause 24 hours before buying.
- Torn? → Split the difference and document it.

This rewires your instincts for generational wealth.

10 Journal Prompts for Chapter Four: Wealth Flow Psychology

1. Am I more naturally an Egg Hoarder or a Dino Giver—and why?
2. What am I afraid will happen if I invest money in myself?
3. What am I afraid will happen if I *don't* spend money?
4. Where do I overshare my time, energy, or finances?
5. Where do I under-share or withhold value?
6. What patterns from my childhood affect my wealth flow today?
7. What does wealth "feel" like to me—heavy, dangerous, exciting, or freeing?
8. What part of wealth flow feels the most difficult for me to master?
9. What is one small daily money habit that would transform my life?
10. If I trusted myself completely, what financial decision would I make this week?

Closing Reflection for Chapter Four

You now understand the ancient instincts that govern your wealth behavior—your hoarding fear and your giving impulse. Neither one is wrong. Neither one is a flaw. Both are evolutionary masterpieces designed to protect and empower you.

But you are not living in the prehistoric world anymore.

You're building an **empire**.

And an empire requires strategic flow, not instinctual extremes.

You learned that money moves like water, like blood, like energy—it must circulate, evolve, and grow. You discovered that wealth isn't something you force into existence; it's something you **balance**, **channel**, and **direct**.

You are no longer trapped in outdated financial instincts.

You are now aligned with evolutionary wealth psychology.

You are becoming someone who moves money with confidence, purpose, and clarity.

In Chapter Five, you take everything you have learned—your instincts, your strengths, your business bones, your wealth flow—and carve it into something unforgettable:

A **brand with bite**, a mark that endures, and a presence that dominates the modern landscape.

Your evolution continues.

Chapter Five – Building a Brand with Bite

When prehistoric creatures wanted to survive, they grew armor.
When they wanted to dominate, they grew teeth.

Your brand is your armor *and* your teeth.
It protects your ideas—and it leaves a mark on the world.

A brand with bite is not polite, invisible, or forgettable.
A brand with bite is:

- Recognizable
- Memorable
- Unmistakably YOU
- Built with purpose
- Guided by instinct
- Rooted in ancient psychological patterns of attraction and dominance

Building a brand that thrives today requires evolutionary thinking.
Attention is the new oxygen.
Identity is the new territory.
Perception is the new survival landscape.

This chapter teaches you how to build a brand that carries the resilience of a creature that endured millions of years—while still feeling sharp, modern, magnetic, and profitable.

Your brand is not your logo.
Your brand is not your colors.
Your brand is not your font.

Your brand is the fossil impression you leave behind everywhere you go.
This chapter turns you into the creature that leaves those marks.

What Is a Brand With Bite?

A brand with bite is a brand that:

- **Breaks patterns**
- **Stands out visually, emotionally, and psychologically**
- **Communicates value instantly**
- **Triggers recognition in seconds**
- **Feels like it was carved from your bones**
- **Attracts your ideal audience without force**
- **Holds territory** in its niche

Your brand's bite marks are the emotional impressions left on people after seeing your name, reading your content, experiencing your work, or hearing about you secondhand.

Your bite = your impression.

Your impression = your power.

Your power = your revenue.

The Fossil Identity Framework — Your Brand's Skeleton

Your brand is a skeleton built from five bone groups:

1. Skull – Your Core Message

The skull houses the brain.
Your brand's "skull" is its central idea.

Ask:
What is the ONE sentence my brand stands for?

Examples:

- "Your instincts can make you rich."
- "Your past does not determine your wealth."
- "Transformation begins with remembering who you are."

Everything else—design, content, marketing—must align with your skull.

2. Spine – Your Values and Personality
The spine holds your brand together.
Your values shape your:

- Tone
- Boundaries
- Audience
- Content themes
- Emotional impact

Examples of spine values:

- Strength
- Clarity
- Evolution
- Power
- Resilience
- Truth
- Efficiency
- Momentum

A brand with no spine collapses.
A brand with a strong spine stands tall in any market.

3. Ribs – Your Main Offers and Creations

Just like ribs protect vital organs, your main offers are the heart of your business.

These include:

- Books
- Courses
- Templates
- Digital products
- Merchandise
- Coaching
- Memberships

Your ribs must protect what matters most: **your income structure**.

4. Teeth – Your Market Differentiation

Teeth represent:

- Sharp messaging
- Boldness
- Uniqueness
- Positioning
- Advantages

Your teeth are what make people pay attention.

Ask:

What makes my brand dangerous to obscurity?

(What makes me impossible to ignore?)

Examples of "teeth":

- A primal theme
- Standout titles
- Unique metaphors
- Evolutionary branding
- Cursive silver signature
- Aggressive clarity
- Brutal honesty
- Hyper-productive output

Without teeth, your brand cannot bite—and cannot dominate.

5. Legs – Your Consistency and Movement

Your brand must move.

A brand that stands still becomes fossilized in the wrong way—forgotten.

Movement includes:

- Posting
- Publishing
- Creating
- Updating
- Reinforcing your identity
- Showing up regularly
- Expanding your territory

Your legs create momentum.

Your momentum builds empire.

The Predator Positioning Method — Claiming Your Niche Territory

In prehistoric ecosystems, predators never fought every creature—they picked a habitat and ruled it.

The same is true in business.

Your brand must:

- Choose its territory
- Define its prey (your audience)
- Claim its land
- Mark its presence

Your territory is your niche.

Your "hunt" is your ideal customer.

Your "dominance" is your positioning.

This is **Predator Positioning**, and it works like this:

1. Identify the problem your brand solves
2. Identify the emotional gap your audience feels
3. Identify the promise only YOU can make
4. Identify the transformation your brand delivers
5. Communicate all four things consistently

Territory claimed.

Competitors eliminated.

Recognition achieved.

The Bite Blueprint – Making Your Brand Unforgettable

A brand becomes unforgettable when it contains these five evolutionary triggers:

1. Familiarity

The brain remembers repeated patterns.
Your brand must look and sound similar across all platforms.

2. Novelty

The brain notices differences.
Your titles, imagery, and metaphors must break patterns.

3. Emotion

People remember how you made them feel.
Your brand should evoke something primal—hope, confidence, power, hunger.

4. Identity

Your brand must represent a version of your audience they want to become.

5. Marking

Every creature marks territory.
Your brand must leave a trace:

- Cursive silver signature
- Distinct color palette
- Recognizable titles
- Consistent voice
- Prehistoric metaphors

These become your "bite marks."

The Brand Construction Ritual — A Guided Building Process

Below is a full-step exercise to build your brand's identity using your primal instincts.

STEP 1: Your Brand Skull (Core Message)

Answer:

What is the one idea my brand wants to put into the world?

STEP 2: Your Brand Spine (Values & Personality)

Choose 3–5 brand values that fit your nature:

- Strength
- Evolution
- Wealth
- Precision
- Honesty
- Creativity
- Discipline
- Protection

Write yours:

STEP 3: Your Brand's Teeth (Differentiation)

What makes you unique?

List 5 things you do differently:

These are your bite marks.

STEP 4: Your Brand Ribs (Offers)
List your main products:

- Books
- Templates
- Coaching
- YouTube content
- Guides
- Digital courses
- PDFs

Write your core offers:

STEP 5: Your Brand Legs (Movement Strategy)
Choose your movement:

- Daily content
- Weekly videos
- Monthly book drops
- Systematic publishing

Write your rhythm:
This is your motion system.

Sharpening Your Ancient Decision-Making Tools to Build a Brand

Your ancestors made decisions based on:

- Pattern recognition
- Energy conservation
- Risk calculation
- Territory management
- Identity reinforcement
- Environmental assessment

Use the same logic:

Before creating anything, ask:

1. Does this fit my skull (core message)?
2. Does this strengthen my spine (values)?
3. Does this sharpen my teeth (stand out)?
4. Does this protect my ribs (offers)?
5. Does this move my legs (momentum)?

If yes → create.
If no → discard.

Evolution never wastes energy.
Neither should you.

The Empire Formula — Building a Brand That Survives Millions of Years

Empires are built by:

- Identity
- Clarity
- Precision
- Repetition
- Adaptability
- Resilience

Your brand must evolve, but never lose its skeleton.

You rebuild, expand, strengthen, and update—
but your bones remain the same.

That is how creatures survived.

That is how brands dominate.

10 Journal Prompts for Chapter Five: Building a Brand with Bite

1. What emotions do I want people to feel when they encounter my brand?
2. What is the single message my brand must deliver every time?
3. What makes my brand visually and emotionally unique?
4. What values will I never compromise on?
5. What colors, symbols, or metaphors feel primal and aligned with my message?
6. What "bite marks" do I want to leave across platforms?
7. How will my brand move consistently each week?
8. What offers do I want at the core of my brand?
9. What should my brand never do because it goes against my instincts?
10. What will my brand be known for 10 years from now?

Closing Reflection

You have spent the first four chapters excavating your value, mapping your instincts, understanding your traps, and balancing your wealth flow. Now, all of that ancient intelligence comes together to shape your identity—your brand, your presence, your voice.

A brand with bite is not something you create.
It is something you **reveal**—a creature formed from your strengths, your purpose, your message, and your primal design.

Millions of people build brands that vanish.
A small few build brands that endure.
And an even smaller, rarer group builds brands that dominate.

You now have the tools to join that rare group.

Your brand has bones.
Your brand has identity.
Your brand has bite.

In your hands lies the power to create something long-lasting, unforgettable, and evolution-strong.

Your prehistoric potential has awakened...
And your empire is just beginning.

Appendix A – Dino Empire Planner

The Dino Empire Planner is your command center—your field journal, excavation map, and empire-building blueprint all in one. It transforms everything you've learned throughout this book into **daily, practical, measurable actions**. This planner is designed like a living organism: it adapts, evolves, and grows with you. It carries the instincts of ancient creatures and the structure of modern business strategy.

This appendix gives you a **full 31-day planner**, weekly empire-building rituals, decision frameworks, and tracking systems—all grounded in the themes of evolution, resilience, instinct, and wealth expansion.

Use this planner to take the bones you unearthed in the earlier chapters...

and assemble them into a thriving, breathing, unstoppable empire.

The Dinosaur Empire Mindset

Before you start planning, you must adopt the psychology of a prehistoric ruler:

1. Move with Purpose

Every creature that thrived did so because every movement had meaning. No wasted steps. No wasted energy.

2. Grow a Layer at a Time

Your empire is built the same way a dinosaur grew: cell by cell, action by action, day after day.

3. Protect Your Territory

Your time, creativity, focus, and energy are sacred land. Not everyone gets access.

4. Expand Through Instinct, Not Fear

Every entry in this planner helps you tie modern business decisions to ancient survival intelligence.

5. Build for Longevity

Fast success burns out.
Evolution-based success endures for generations.

Your Empire Blueprint

This is your 5-part empire skeleton. Fill this out first.

A. The Skull – Your Empire's Core Message

What is the message your entire brand and business stands for?

B. The Spine – Your Core Values

List 3–5 values your empire will never compromise:

C. The Ribs – Your Main Income Streams

Choose your three ribcage revenue streams from the 12 in Chapter 1:

D. The Teeth – Your Differentiators

List five things that make your empire unique—your bite marks:

E. The Legs – Your Weekly Action System

Describe how your empire will move:

Daily rhythm: ____

Weekly rhythm: ____

Monthly rhythm: ____

Weekly Dino Empire Rituals

Every week contains these three rituals. They keep your empire alive and evolving.

1. The Alpha Scan (Every Monday)

Scan your territory (your entire life/business). Write:

- What threats or obstacles do I need to eliminate?
- What opportunities appeared that I must act on?
- What revenue-producing tasks are most important this week?

2. The Fossil Forge (Mid-Week Creation Session)

Choose one thing to create **every week**:

- A book chapter
- A new digital product
- A new piece of content
- A new idea or concept
- A new system

Creation = expansion.
Write your weekly creation goal:

3. The Predator Review (Every Sunday)

Track how you strategically moved toward your goals.
Answer:

- What did I execute?
- What did I avoid?
- Where did instinct guide me?
- Where did fear interfere?

End each week with a victory list of at least 3 wins.

31-Day Dino Empire Planner

This 31-day cycle rewires your instincts, your habits, and your wealth psychology.

Every day contains:

- A movement task
- A creation task
- A financial action
- A mindset ritual

Below is the full framework. You can reuse this every month.

WEEK 1 – Excavation Week
Goal: Uncover instincts, fears, strengths, and hidden potential.

Day 1 – Instinct Scan
Identify 5 instincts that make you powerful.

Day 2 – Fear Extraction
Write down every fear that slows your wealth building.

Day 3 – Strength Mapping
List everything you're good at—even the weird things.
Day 4 – Income Match
Assign each strength to at least one income stream.

Day 5 – Energy Rhythm Discovery
Track your natural productive hours.

Day 6 – Territory Clearing
Remove 1–3 distractions from your weekly life.

Day 7 – Empire Vision Casting
Write the version of yourself that exists 90 days from now.

WEEK 2 – Construction Week
Goal: Build the first bones of your business and brand.

Day 8 – Brand Skull Creation
Write your core message—your empire's "brain."

Day 9 – Spine Strengthening
Define 3–5 brand values.

Day 10 – Ribcage Selection
Choose your three core income streams.

Day 11 – Teeth Sharpening
List your differentiators. Make them bold.

Day 12 – Movement System Design
Create your daily/weekly action rhythm.

Day 13 – Brand Identity Ritual
Choose colors, tone, imagery, and voice.

Day 14 – Empire Map
Sketch your entire business structure on one page.

WEEK 3 – Expansion Week
Goal: Create, publish, produce, and release new assets.

Day 15 – Create 1 New Asset
(book page, video, product, template)

Day 16 – Publish Something
Post or launch a piece of content.

Day 17 – Product Development
Enhance a current asset.

Day 18 – Visibility Ritual
Post 2–3 times on social platforms.

Day 19 – Audience Connection
Engage with followers or readers.

Day 20 – Collaboration Hunt
Reach out to 1 person for partnership.

Day 21 – Mini-Launch
Promote something deliberately.

WEEK 4 – Domination Week
Goal: Strength, endurance, confidence, and income flow.

Day 22 – Wealth Audit
Track all income, spend, and growth.

Day 23 – Debt Dominance Check-In
Apply the Tar Pit escape methods.

Day 24 – System Upgrade
Improve one process.

Day 25 – Offer Strengthening
Enhance a book, product, or system.

Day 26 – Market Bite Increase
Add something bold to your brand.

Day 27 – Territory Expansion
Publish something new or reach new audiences.

Day 28 – Power Ritual
Celebrate wins, growth, and instincts.

DAY 29, 30, 31 – Evolution Days
Goal: Reflect, transform, rest strategically, and evolve.

Day 29 – Reflection Day
What worked, what didn't, what changed?

Day 30 – Integration Day
Absorb lessons from the month.

Day 31 – Reset Day
Plan the next 31-day cycle.

Dino Empire Tracking Sheets

Use these tracking sheets monthly.

Daily Instinct Score (0–10)

Rate each instinct:

- Focus
- Energy
- Confidence
- Creativity
- Discipline
- Clarity

Empire Action Score

Did you:

- Create something today?
- Move your business forward?
- Do one wealth-building action?
- Post something?
- Protect your territory (boundaries)?

Track daily wins here:

Offer Growth Tracker

Offer/ Product	Date Added	Improve-ments	Sales	Notes

Closing Reflection

Your empire is not built in bursts.
It is built in **cycles**—consistent, instinct-guided, strategic cycles.

The Dino Empire Planner is your roadmap, your ritual, and your evolutionary guide. This planner turns every day into an opportunity to grow, strengthen, and expand—without burnout, without confusion, and without fighting your nature.

You now hold the tools to:

- Build an empire with bones
- Move like a predator
- Grow like a creature of resilience
- Expand like a ruler of ancient terrain
- Operate from instinct, not fear
- Build wealth that lasts generations

Your empire will not be accidental.
It will be **engineered**—by you, by your instincts, and by your evolutionary power.

And now...
your next 31 days begin.
Your empire is waiting.

Message from the Author:

I hope you enjoyed this book, I love astrology and knew there was not a book such as this out on the shelf. I love metaphysical items as well. Please check out my other books:

-Life of Government Benefits

-My life of Hell

-My life with Hydrocephalus

-Red Sky

-World Domination:Woman's rule

-World Domination:Woman's Rule 2: The War

-Life and Banishment of Apophis: book 1

-The Kidney Friendly Diet

-The Ultimate Hemp Cookbook

-Creating a Dispensary(legally)

-Cleanliness throughout life: the importance of showering from childhood to adulthood.

-Strong Roots: The Risks of Overcoddling children

-Hemp Horoscopes: Cosmic Insights and Earthly Healing

- Celestial Hemp Navigating the Zodiac: Through the Green Cosmos

-Astrological Hemp: Aligning The Stars with Earth's Ancient Herb

-The Astrological Guide to Hemp: Stars, Signs, and Sacred Leaves

-Green Growth: Innovative Marketing Strategies for your Hemp Products and Dispensary

-Cosmic Cannabis

-Astrological Munchies

-Henry The Hemp

-Zodiacal Roots: The Astrological Soul Of Hemp

- **Green Constellations: Intersection of Hemp and Zodiac**

-Hemp in The Houses: An astrological Adventure Through The Cannabis Galaxy

-Galactic Ganja Guide

Heavenly Hemp

Zodiac Leaves
Doctor Who Astrology
Cannastrology
Stellar Satvias and Cosmic Indicas
Celestial Cannabis: A Zodiac Journey
AstroHerbology: The Sky and The Soil: Volume 1
AstroHerbology:Celestial Cannabis:Volume 2
Cosmic Cannabis Cultivation
The Starry Guide to Herbal Harmony: Volume 1
The Starry Guide to Herbal Harmony: Cannabis Universe: Volume 2
Yugioh Astrology: Astrological Guide to Deck, Duels and more
Nightmare Mansion: Echoes of The Abyss
Nightmare Mansion 2: Legacy of Shadows
Nightmare Mansion 3: Shadows of the Forgotten
Nightmare Mansion 4: Echoes of the Damned
The Life and Banishment of Apophis: Book 2
Nightmare Mansion: Halls of Despair
Healing with Herb: Cannabis and Hydrocephalus
Planetary Pot: Aligning with Astrological Herbs: Volume 1
Fast Track to Freedom: 30 Days to Financial Independence Using AI, Assets, and Agile Hustles
Cosmic Hemp Pathways
How to Become Financially Free in 30 Days: 10,000 Paths to Prosperity
Zodiacal Herbage: Astrological Insights: Volume 1
Nightmare Mansion: Whispers in the Walls
The Daleks Invade Atlantis
Henry the hemp and Hydrocephalus

10X The Kidney Friendly Diet
Cannabis Universe: Adult coloring book
Hemp Astrology: The Healing Power of the Stars

Zodiacal Herbage: Astrological Insights: Cannabis Universe: Volume 2

Planetary Pot: Aligning with Astrological Herbs: Cannabis Universes: Volume 2

Doctor Who: Convergence Protocol – The Replicator War

Nightmare Mansion: Curse of the Blood Moon

The Celestial Stoner: A Guide to the Zodiac

Cosmic Pleasures: Sex Toy Astrology for Every Sign

Hydrocephalus Astrology: Navigating the Stars and Healing Waters

Lapis and the Mischievous Chocolate Bar

Celestial Positions: Sexual Astrology for Every Sign

Apophis's Shadow Work Journal: **:** A Journey of Self-Discovery and Healing

Kinky Cosmos: Sexual Kink Astrology for Every Sign

Digital Cosmos: The Astrological Digimon Compendium

Stellar Seeds: The Cosmic Guide to Growing with Astrology

Apophis's Daily Gratitude Journal

Cat Astrology: Feline Mysteries of the Cosmos

The Cosmic Kama Sutra: An Astrological Guide to Sexual Positions

Unleash Your Potential: A Guided Journal Powered by AI Insights

Whispers of the Enchanted Grove

Cosmic Pleasures: An Astrological Guide to Sexual Kinks

369, 12 Manifestation Journal

Whisper of the nocturne journal(blank journal for writing or drawing)

The Boogey Book

Locked In Reflection: A Chastity Journey Through Locktober

Generating Wealth Quickly:How to Generate $100,000 in 24 Hours

Star Magic: Harness the Power of the Universe

The Flatulence Chronicles: A Fart Journal for Self-Discovery

The Doctor and The Death Moth

Seize the Day: A Personal Seizure Tracking Journal

The Ultimate Boogeyman Safari: A Journey into the Boogie World and Beyond

Whispers of Samhain: 1,000 Spells of Love, Luck, and Lunar Magic: Samhain Spell Book

Apophis's guides:Witch's Spellbook Crafting Guide for Halloween

Frost & Flame: The Enchanted Yule Grimoire of 1000 Winter Spells

The Ultimate Boogey Goo Guide & Spooky Activities for Halloween Fun

Harmony of the Scales: A Libra's Spellcraft for Balance and Beauty

The Enchanted Advent: 36 Days of Christmas Wonders

Nightmare Mansion: The Labyrinth of Screams

Harvest of Enchantment: 1,000 Spells of Gratitude, Love, and Fortune for Thanksgiving

The Boogey Chronicles: A Journal of Nightly Encounters and Shadowy Secrets

The 12 Days of Financial Freedom: A Step-by-Step Christmas Countdown to Transform Your Finances

Sigil of the Eternal Spiral Blank Journal

A Christmas Feast: Timeless Recipes for Every Meal

Holiday Stress-Free Solutions: A Survival Guide to Thriving During the Festive Season

Yu-Gi-Oh! Holiday Gifting Mastery: The Ultimate Guide for Fans and Newcomers Alike

Holiday Harmony: A Hydrocephalus Survival Guide for the Festive Season

Celestial Craft: The Witch's Almanac for 2025 – A Cosmic Guide to Manifestations, Moons, and Mystical Events

Doctor Who: The Toymaker's Winter Wonderland

Tulsa King Unveiled: A Thrilling Guide to Stallone's Mafia Masterpiece

Pendulum Craft: A Complete Guide to Crafting and Using Personalized Divination Tools

Nightmare Mansion: Santa's Eternal Eve

Starlight Noel: A Cosmic Journey through Christmas Mysteries

The Dark Architect: Unlocking the Blueprint of Existence

Surviving the Embrace: The Ultimate Guide to Encounters with The Hugging Molly

The Enchanted Codex: Secrets of the Craft for Witches, Wiccans, and Pagans

Harvest of Gratitude: A Complete Thanksgiving Guide

Yuletide Essentials: A Complete Guide to an Authentic and Magical Christmas

Celestial Smokes: A Cosmic Guide to Cigars and Astrology

Living in Balance: A Comprehensive Survival Guide to Thriving with Diabetes Insipidus

Cosmic Symbiosis: The Venom Zodiac Chronicles

The Cursed Paw of Ambition

Cosmic Symbiosis: The Astrological Venom Journal

Celestial Wonders Unfold: A Stargazer's Guide to the Cosmos (2024-2029)

The Ultimate Black Friday Prepper's Guide: Mastering Shopping Strategies and Savings

Cosmic Sales: The Astrological Guide to Black Friday Shopping

Legends of the Corn Mother and Other Harvest Myths

Whispers of the Harvest: The Corn Mother's Journal

The Evergreen Spellbook

The Doctor Meets the Boogeyman

The White Witch of Rose Hall's SpellBook

The Gingerbread Golem's Shadow: A Study in Sweet Darkness

The Gingerbread Golem Codex: An Academic Exploration of Sweet Myths

The Gingerbread Golem Grimoire: Sweet Magicks and Spells for the Festive Witch

The Curse of the Gingerbread Golem

10-minute Christmas Crafts for kids

Christmas Crisis Solutions: The Ultimate Last-Minute Survival Guide

Gingerbread Golem Recipes: Holiday Treats with a Magical Twist

The Infinite Key: Unlocking Mystical Secrets of the Ages

Enchanted Yule: A Wiccan and Pagan Guide to a Magical and Memorable Season

Dinosaurs of Power: Unlocking Ancient Magick

Astro-Dinos: The Cosmic Guide to Prehistoric Wisdom

Gallifrey's Yule Logs: A Festive Doctor Who Cookbook

The Dino Grimoire: Secrets of Prehistoric Magick

The Gift They Never Knew They Needed

The Gingerbread Golem's Culinary Alchemy: Enchanting Recipes for a Sweetly Dark Feast

A Time Lord Christmas: Holiday Adventures with the Doctor

Krampusproofing Your Home: Defensive Strategies for Yule

Silent Frights: A Collection of Christmas Creepypastas to Chill Your Bones

Santa Raptor's Jolly Carnage: A Dino-Claus Christmas Tale

Prehistoric Palettes: A Dino Wicca Coloring Journey

The Christmas Wishkeeper Chronicles

The Starlight Sleigh: A Holiday Journey

Elf Secrets: The True Magic of the North Pole

Candy Cane Conjurations

Cooking with Kids: Recipes Under 20 Minutes

Doctor Who: The TARDIS Confiscation

The Anxiety First Aid Kit: Quick Tools to Calm Your Mind

Frosty Whispers: A Winter's Tale

The Infinite Key: Unlocking the Secrets to Prosperity, Resilience, and Purpose

The Grasping Void: Why You'll Regret This Purchase

Astrology for Busy Bees: Star Signs Simplified

The Instant Focus Formula: Cut Through the Noise

The Secret Language of Colors: Unlocking the Emotional Codes

Sacred Fossil Chronicles: Blank Journal

The Christmas Cottage Miracle

Feeding Frenzy: Graboid-Inspired Recipes

Manifest in Minutes: The Quick Law of Attraction Guide

The Symbiote Chronicles: Doctor Who's Venomous Journey

Think Tiny, Grow Big: The Minimalist Mindset

The Energy Key: Unlocking Limitless Motivation

New Year, New Magic: Manifesting Your Best Year Yet

Unstoppable You: Mastering Confidence in Minutes

Infinite Energy: The Secret to Never Feeling Drained

Lightning Focus: Mastering the Art of Productivity in a Distracted World

Saturnalia Manifestation Magick: A Guide to Unlocking Abundance During the Solstice

Graboids and Garland: The Ultimate Tremors-Themed Christmas Guide

12 Nights of Holiday Magic

The Power of Pause: 60-Second Mindfulness Practices

The Quick Reset: How to Reclaim Your Life After Burnout

The Shadow Eater: A Tale of Despair and Survival

The Micro-Mastery Method: Transform Your Skills in Just Minutes a Day

Reclaiming Time: How to Live More by Doing Less

Chronovore: The Eternal Nexus

The Mind Reset: Unlocking Your Inner Peace in a Chaotic World

Confidence Code: Building Unshakable Self-Belief

Baby the Vampire Terrier
Baby the Vampire Terrier's Christmas Adventure
Celestial Streams: The Content Creator's Astrology Manual
The Wealth Whisperer: Unlocking Abundance with Everyday Actions
The Energy Equation: Maximize Your Output Without Burning Out
The Happiness Algorithm: Science-Backed Steps to Joyful Living
Stress-Free Success: Achieving Goals Without Anxiety
Mindful Wealth: The New Blueprint for Financial Freedom
The Festive Flavors of New Year: A Culinary Celebration
The Master's Gambit: Keys of Eternal Power
Shadowed Secrets: Groundhog Day Mysteries
Beneath the Burrow: Lessons from the Groundhog
Spring's Whispers: The Groundhog's Prediction
The Limitless Mindset: Unlock Your Untapped Potential
The Focus Funnel: How to Cut Through Chaos and Get Results
Bold Moves: Building Courage to Live on Your Terms
The Daily Shift: Simple Practices for Lasting Transformation
The Quarter-Life Reset: Thriving in Your 20s and 30s
The Art of Shadowplay: Building Your Own Personal Myth
The Eternal Loop: Finding Purpose in Repetition
Burrowing Wisdom: Life Lessons from the Groundhog
Shadow Work: A Groundhog Day Perspective
Love in Bloom: 5-Minute Romantic Gestures
The Shadowspell Codex: Secrets of Forbidden Magick
The Burnout Cure: Finding Balance in a Busy World
The Groundhog Prophecy: Unlocking Seasonal Secrets
Nog Tales: The Spirited History of Eggnog
Six More Weeks: Embracing Seasonal Transitions
The Lumivian Chronicles: Fragments of the Fifth Dimension
Money on Your Mind: A Beginner's Guide to Wealth
The Focus Fix: Breaking Through Distraction

January's Spirit Keepers: Mystical Protectors of the Cold
Creativity Unchained: Unlocking Your Wildest Ideas in 2025
Manifestation Mastery: 365 Days to Rewrite Your Reality
The Groundhog's Mirror: Reflecting on Change
The Weeping Angels' Christmas Curse
Burrowed in Time: A Groundhog Day Journey
Heartbeats: Poems to Share with Your Valentine
Dino Wicca: The Sacred Grimoire of Prehistoric Magick
Courage of the Pride: Finding Your Inner Roar
The Lion's Leap: Bold Moves for Big Results
Healthy Hustle: Achieving Without Overworking
Practical Manifesting: Turning Dreams into Reality in 2025
Jurassic Pharaohs: Unlocking the Magick of Ancient Egypt and Dino Wicca
The Happiness Equation: Small Changes for Big Joy
The Confidence Compass: Finding Your Inner Strength
Whispers in the Hollow: Tales of the Forgotten Beasts
Echoes from the Hollow: The Return of Forgotten Beasts
The Hollow Ascendant: The Rise of the Forgotten Beasts
The Relationship Reset: Building Better Connections
Mastering the Morning: How to Win the Day Before 8 AM
The Shadow's Dance: Groundhog Day Symbolism
Cupid's Kitchen: Quick Valentine's Day Recipes
Valentine's Day on a Budget: Love Without Breaking the Bank
Astrocraft: Aligning the Stars in the World of Minecraft
Forecasting Life: Groundhog Day Reflections

Bleeding Hearts: Twisted Tales of Valentine's Terror

Herbal Smoke Revolution: The Ultimate Guide to Nature's Cigarette Alternative

Winter's Wrath: The Complete Survival Blueprint for Extreme Freezes.

The Groundhog's Shadow: A Tale of Seasons
Burrowed Insights: Wisdom from the Groundhog

Sensual Strings: The Art of Erotic Bondage
Whispered Flames: Unlocking the Power of Fire Play
Forgotten Shadows: A Guide to Cryptids Lost to Time
Six Weeks of Secrets: Groundhog Day's Hidden Messages
Shadows and Cycles: Groundhog Day Reflections
The Art of Love Letters: Crafting the Perfect Message
Romantic Getaways at Home: Turning Your Space into Paradise
Purrfect Brews: A Cat Lover's Guide to Coffee and Companionship
The Groundhog's Wisdom: Timeless Lessons for Modern Life
The Shadow Oracle: Groundhog Day as a Predictor
Emerging from the Burrow: A Journey of Renewal
The Language of Love: Learning Your Partner's Love Style
Authorpreneur: The Ultimate Blueprint for Writing, Publishing, and Thriving as an Author
Weathering the Seasons: Groundhog Day Perspectives
Valentine's Day Magic: A Guide to Romantic Rituals
The Shadow Chronicles: Stories of Groundhog Day
Love and Laughter: Fun Games for Valentine's Day
AstroRealty: Unlocking the Stars for Property Success
The Groundhog's Path: A Guide to Seasonal Balance
Groundhog Day Diaries: Reflections in the Shadow
The Groundhog's Light: Illuminating the Path Ahead
Valentine's Traditions from Around the World
AI Wealth Revolution: Unlocking the Trillionaire Mindset
Love Rekindled: Reigniting Passion in Relationships
Single and Thriving: Self-Love on Valentine's Day
Emerald Legends: Mystical Tales of Ireland
Green Alchemy: Harnessing Nature's Magic
The Hearts of Horror: A Valentine's Day Nightmare
The Leprechaun's Guide to Wealth and Wisdom
Dancing with the Sidhe: Celebrating the Otherworld

Shamrocks and Shadows: Mysteries of the Green Isle

Emerald Energy: Harnessing Luck and Growth

The Gingerbread Golem's Valentine: A Sweetheart's Guide to Love and Enchantment

The Celtic Knot: Weaving Life and Destiny

Green Fire: Elemental Magic for St. Patrick's Day

Clover Chronicles: Finding Your Inner Luck

Ireland's Mystical Creatures: A Field Guide

Gingerbread Golem's Love Almanac

Prowl and Thrive: The Lion's Guide to Success

Love Alchemy: Transforming Your Life Through Heart Energy

WORLD DOMINATION: Woman's Rule 3:The New Life

The Midnight Rose: A Guide to Lunar Love Spells

The Forbidden Letters: Writing Your Own Love Prophecy

Luck and Lore: St. Patrick's Day for Modern Mystics

The Green Path: A Pagan Celebration of Renewal

The Dark Architect's Guide to Reprogramming Reality

Prankster's Paradise: A Guide to Harmless Hijinks

Manifest Your Reality: The Law of Attraction Simplified

The TARDIS Owner's Manual: Understanding the Doctor's Ship: *A complete guide to the TARDIS, its technology, secrets, and mysteries*

Starlit Romance: Astrology Secrets for Finding True Love

The Time Lord's Atlas: A Complete Guide to the Whoniverse: ***A breakdown of the locations, planets, and dimensions explored in Doctor Who***

Sweetheart Shadows: The Dark Side of Love and Attraction

February Fire: Reigniting Passion in Every Area of Life

The Self-Love Toolkit: 5 Ways to Embrace Who You Are

February Sparks: Ignite Your Dreams in 28 Days

March to Success: A 31-Day Action Blueprint

Ancient Paths: The 13 Sacred Principles of Dino Wicca

Echoes of Tomorrow: Navigating the AI Revolution
The Wellness Blueprint: Balancing Mind, Body, and Soul
Green Horizons: Sustainable Living for a Better Tomorrow
The AI Wealth Code: How to Make Millions with Automation
AI-Powered Creativity: Writing, Art, and Music for Profit
Extinction Rites: Rebirthing Your Soul Through Prehistoric Magick
Sacred Serpents tarot
Celestial Enchantment blank journal
Star Strains
Culinary Journeys: Exploring Global Flavors at Home
The Hollowvale Curse
The Hollowvale Harvest
The Egg of Transformation: Awakening Your Inner Power
Blooming Into Power: A Wiccan Guide to Spring Awakening
The Nightmare Nexus: The Third Doctor's Perilous Haunting
Digital Detox: Reclaiming Your Life in a Connected World
Ostara's Path: Walking the Spiral of Renewal
The Sacred Hare
Financial Freedom: Building Wealth in the Modern Age
Spring's Cauldron: Stirring the Waters of Change
The Hollowvale Pact
Quantum Consciousness: The Science of Reality Shifting
The Hollowvale Hunger
The Sacred Waters Within: A Witch's Guide to Hydrocephalus Magick
The Raven's Nest: Building a Life of Unshakable Stability
AI and the Human Mind: The Future of Intelligence
The Hollowvale Reckoning
Timeless Love: Building and Maintaining Lasting Relationships
The Raven's Roar: Unlocking Unstoppable Confidence
Raven Sight: Awakening Intuition and Inner Wisdom

The Butterfly Effect: Small Changes, Big Transformations
Taming the Boogeyman: How to Conquer Your Inner Fears
The Magick of Green: Awakening Earth's Energy in You
The Entrepreneurial Mindset: Secrets to Business Success
The Hollowvale End
The Shadow Luck Ritual: Reclaiming Power from Your Dark Side
Spring Magick for Beginners: A Simple Guide to Seasonal Energy Work
Doctor Who: The Hollowvale Conundrum
The March of Miracles: Unlocking Synchronicities in Spring
Unveiling the Cosmos: A Guide to Stargazing and Space Exploration
The Ultimate Guide to Surviving an Economic Collapse
The AI Gold Rush: How to Profit from the AI Revolution
Bastet's Shadow: The Hidden Power of Feline Magick
The Bastet Codex: Unlocking the Goddess's Magickal Secrets
Purring Spells: Harnessing Bastet's Healing Frequencies
Bastet's Nine Lives: Rebirth, Transformation, and Immortality Spells
Primal Currents: Hydrocephalus Magick in the Path of Dino Wicca
The Digital Gold Rush: Mastering E-Commerce and Online Sales
Future Shock: Adapting to the Next Decade of Change
The Quantum Mindset: Think Like a Billionaire
Sacred Motherhood: Awakening the Divine Feminine Within
The Mother's Spellbook: Enchantments for Love, Protection, and Prosperity
The Witch's Guide to Parenting: Raising Empowered and Intuitive Children
The Magick of Motherhood: Reclaiming Your Power Through Rituals

The Pagan Path to Self-Love: A Goddess's Guide to Worth and Confidence
Wild Woman Magick: Unleashing Your Primal Power
The Money Magnet Blueprint: Unlocking Unlimited Wealth
Biohacking 101: Unlock Your Body's Full Potential
The Wild Father: A Pagan Guide to Strength and Wisdom
The Sacred Masculine: Unlocking Your Inner Power
The Druid's Compass
The Warrior's Mindset
The Father's Fire
Odin's Path
Ancestral Bonds
The House That Whispers
The Magician's Code
The Wild Hunt
The Green Man's Path
The Altar of Success
The Shadow and the Sword
The High Priestess's Guide to Energy Healing
The Lunar Mother
The Sacred Self-Care Grimoire
The Womb Wisdom Codex
The Wheel of the Mother
The Witch's Guide to Manifestation
The Q2 Reset
The Ultimate Guide to AI-Powered Passive Income
Escape the 9-5
AI Feline Fortunes
The Tear-Stained Grimoire
Razorblade Runes
Cemetery Sirens
The Midnight Wristwatch
The Town That Forgets

AI Horror & Creepypasta
The Hollow Frequency
The Breach Echo
The Quiet Between Worlds
The Sigil of Tharan-Khul
Summon the Vault of Y'ha'ten
The Becoming Codex
The Profit of Az'ra-nar
The Drowned Logos
Echoes of the Eldritch Will
The Deep Ledger
Necronomicon of Networth
Covenant of the Wealthwyrm
The Whisperer's Manifesto
The Rites of Azh-K'luth
The Ark of the Crawling Coin
The Tithe of Shadows
Inkheart Abyss
The Timewinds of Y'ha-nthlei
The Spiral Labyrinth of Azag-Nirrh
The Gallifreyan Heresy of the Black Pharaoh
The Psalms of Nyog-Sotha
Black Rain Alchemy
The Infinite Maw
The Entropic Blueprint
The Oracle of Sh'guul
The Book of Breach
The Drowned Saint's Testament
Dreamcraft of the Sleeper God
The Silence Market
Cthonomics: The Dark Wealth Algorithm
Invocation of the Ten-Eyed King
Wealthbound to the Wyrm Below

Become the Unnameable
Codex of the Sovereign Flame
Rituals of Relentless Becoming
The Shadow Ascends
The Eyes Beneath You
The Will That Wakes Worlds
Silence Is a Weapon
The Mirror That Screams
The Whisper Between Moments
The Mind That Devours Fear
The Myth of the Finished Self
The Architect of Your Madness
The Voice You've Buried
The Discipline of Madness
Stormborn: Awakening Your Inner Tempest
The Mind That Ate Time
Unbind Your Becoming
The Pact You Owe Yourself
The Devourer's Diet
The Acid That Carves the Path
The Tower You Must Burn
The Breath Between Worlds
Speak Like the Deep
The Labyrinth Within
The Spine of the Sea God
Rejection Is a Portal
The Crown You Refused
The Scar Is the Spell
The Lightless Flame
The Habit of Becoming Horrific
ChickenJockey Chaos
The Gatekeeper Within
You Are Not Your Name

The Compass of the Mad
The Archive of Unsent Letters
What the Mirror Can't Show You
The Knife You Needed
Worship Nothing, Become Everything
The Other Voice
The Body the World Forgot
The Vein of the Void
The Black Bone Codex
The Puzzle of the Hidden Self (Millennium Puzzle)
The Eye That Sees the Lie *(Millennium Eye)*
The Ring of Return (Millennium Ring)
The Rod of Relentless Will *(Millennium Rod)*
The Tally of the Soul (Millennium Tauk/Necklace)
The Key to the Locked Timeline (Millennium Key)
The Scale of Sacred Decisions (Millennium Scales)
Inferno Bites: The UnOfficial Minecraft Lava Cookbook
Rot in the Attic
Prana: The Hidden Force of Your Infinite Self
The Shadow Realm Within: Transforming Darkness Into Destiny
The Borderland Collapse
Claws of Protection: Bastet's Defensive Magick
Mr. Ring-a-Ding's Madness
Yugioh Astrology: Celestial Deckcraft and Duel Destiny (2026–2027 Edition)
The Seal You Signed: Unlocking the Power You Once Feared
The Puzzle of Infinite Minds: Unlocking the Mentalism Hidden Within
The Eye That Mirrors the All: Secrets of Inner Reflection
Doctor Who: The Toymaker's Broadcast
The Rod of Eternal Flow: Commanding the Currents of Vibration

Golden Eyes of Bastet: Enhancing Psychic Vision
The Key of Dual Forces: Balance Within the Polarity
The Scales of Living Rhythm: Timing the Dance of Life
The Necklace of Hidden Cause: Weaving the Webs of Fate
The Ring of Secret Masters: Rising Through the All Within All
Daggers of the Dying Deep
Bastet's Wealth and Fortune Magick: Prosperity Rituals of the Goddess
The Tide that Speaks
The Scrolls of Petosiris: 13 Rituals from the Feathered Eye
Petosiris and the Living Plague of Osirion
Feline Fire: Bastet's Passion and Love Magick
The Star Altar of Petosiris
Bastet's Whiskers: Supernatural Sensory Magick
The Bastet Grimoire
Feeding the Shadows
The Mouthless Prayer
The Spiral Wound
Becoming the Ibis: Lessons from Petosiris's Mind
The Crimson Coven: Cola Magick for Sweet Dominion
Sacred Cat's Paw
The Soda Zodiac: A Flavor for Every Sign
Covenant of the Crawling Flame
The Ink of Ish'Zur
Frothroot: The Thirst That Ate the World
The Golden Glyphs of Prosperity
The Etherbind Codex
Echoes of the Resistance: Reclaiming the You That Survived
Harnessed Minds: Breaking Free from Mental Control
The Eyes in the Smoke
Rootwake: The Carbon Covenant
Skitter Logic: Unlearning the Fear That Built You

Doctor Who: The World That Froths
Rootwake: The Fizz That Rewrites Flesh
Rootwake: Frothfather of the World
The Holly Pact: Blood Beneath the Mistletoe
The 2nd Mass Principle: Building Unbreakable Tribes
Web of Wits: A Survival Guide to Encounters with Anasi the Spider (Aunt Nancy)
The Hexbreaking Handbook: Effective Spells to Remove Curses
Pop Alchemy: Transform Your Life One Sip at a Time
The Mason Code: Leading in Unleadable Times
Petosiris and the Fifth Chamber of Thoth
The Ether Seed Within
The Parent of Tomorrow
Petosiris's Pyramid of Perpetual Wealth
Unlearn the World
Grimoire of the Hollow Tongue
Zodiac Weeds: Finding Your Strain Through the Stars
Aquarius Rises in the Bank
The Sugar God's Smile
The Skinclock Reversal: Biohacking the Face of Time
Debtburn: How to Obliterate What You Owe Forever
The Ice Cream Oracle: What Your Cone Says About Your Future
Silence Is Sovereignty: The Power of Being Unreadable
The Wind That Whispers Through Stone
Path of the Four Directions
Doctor Who: The Maestro's Symphony of Endings
Oxygen Grail: Breathing to Undo the Clock
Zodiacal Collapse: When Stars Devour Time
Teachings from the Red Sand Silence
Doctor Who: Omega – The Broken Equation
Memory Wipe Your Past: Start Over Like a MiB

Mitochondria Prime: Ignite the Core of Youth
A Nest of Roaches
Grub from the Galaxy: MiB Recipes You'll Never Forget
Whiskers of Power: Bastet's Guide to Inner Sovereignty
The Gift Must Cost Them: Negotiation Through Unequal Exchange
The Worm Guys' Wealth Code: Hustle Like an Alien
Bug Out: The Edgar Method for Ruthless Goal Setting
Weaving Life with Spiderwoman's Pattern
Doctor Who: The Rani's Renaissance
How to Get a Job (If You're a Puppygirl)
Speak Through Others: The Art of Proxy Power
T-Rex Your Trauma: Reclaim the Power of Your Primal Self
The Black Briefcase: How MiB Stay Wealthy in Silence
The Thirst Beyond Reason: Understanding Diabetes Insipidus From the Inside Out
Backwoods Witchcraft for Billionaires: The Pagan Path from Dirt Roads to Gold Roads
The Moonshine Grimoire: Fermented Spells for Abundance
The Nameless Geometry
The Wraith's Mixtape: Spellcasting with Songs of Sorrow
The Gallifreyan Gentleman: Silent Wealth, Sonic Confidence, and the Doctor's Code of Living
Sugar Water Confidence
Dino Totems: Spirit Guides from Earth's First Gods
Pumpkin Sigils & Ritual Smoke
The Hózhó Compass
The Distortus Discipline – Order from Inner Mutation
Witchcraft for the Cold-Blooded Soul
Moonlight Over the Blessingway
Water, Interrupted: When the Body Forgets How to Hold On
Deformed but Divine: Embracing Your Asymmetry
Hexes in the Henhouse: The Farm Witch's Guide to Power

The Reversed Flame: A Grimoire of Inverted Power

Salt, Cells, and Sanity: Reclaiming Balance with Diabetes Insipidus

King of the Broken: Crowning the Flawed Self

Moonlight Scars: Emo Moon Magick and the Art of Lunar Sorrow

Noose Spells: Magick of the Hanging Rope

The Goth Cathedral: Rituals of the Broken and Beautiful

The Cretaceous Codex: Dino Spirits and Fossil Magick

The Turkey Bones Ritual

Nine Lives of Manifestation: Unlocking Bastet's Reality Codes

Chaos Muscles: Building Strength from Twisted Pain

Emo Blood Magick: The Veins of Power

The 3AM Flood: Nighttime Urination, Sleep Loss, and the DI Spiral

The Silence Between the Stars

The Lemon Method: Sour Your Way to Success

Starlit Sovereign

The Rite of Twelve Gates: Walking the Gates of the Duat.

Cornbread and Conjure: Recipes for Riches and Rootwork

The Black Rose Rituals: Emo Love Spells and Obsession Magick

The Eternal Goodbye: Death Magick and Rebirth Rituals

Sinkrot: The Drain That Remembers

The Hybrid Mindset: Thinking Beyond Evolution

Bone Dry: Navigating Dehydration Before It Breaks You

Wreathcraft: Winter Sigils and Yuletide Spells

The Rite of Twelve Mouths

S'mores of the Damned: Haunted Recipes for Halloween Night

Rethink the Drink: A Beverage Survival Guide for DI Warriors

The Shadow Chord: Guitar Magick and Sonic

Malformed Yet Majestic: Leading When You Feel Wrong Inside

The Cursed Diary: Ink-Stained Spells of the Emo Soul

Anxiety Off Switch: Emergency Reset for a Fried Nervous System

The Energy Heist: How to Take Back Your Life from Drainers

Beyond the Bathroom: Rebuilding Your Social Life With DI

Coyote's Gift for Decision Makers

Ghoul-Goo: Spooky S'mores You'll Die For

Echoes in the Mirror: Scrying and Self-Destruction Magick

Thread and Thorn: Stitching Spells from Rural Cloth

The Mogwai Mind: Building Untouchable Wealth from Small Ideas

Be Your Own Guide: Trust Your Inner Compass

Hormones in Chaos: The Endocrine Puzzle of Diabetes Insipidus

ChronoCleanse: Detox Your Biological Timeline

The Limb You Hide Is the One That Saves You

Leaves, Bones, and Whisper Spells

The Dinosaur Mindset: Prehistoric Tactics for Modern Wealth

Clawing Back Control: A Bastet Method for Boundaries and Empowerment

Samhain Codes of the Forgotten

Orange Alchemy: The Autumnal Spellbook

Monster Within, Master Without

The Sigil That Sleeps

Hearthcraft: Yule Hearth Sigils and Winter Warmth Spells

Temple of the Purring Moon: Rituals from Bastet's Lineage

When the Earth Remembers Your Footsteps

Food for Mood: Eat to Heal Depression, Not Just Survive It

Witch of the Kudzu Vine: Southern Pagan Wealth Secrets

The Invisible Diagnosis: Advocating for Yourself With DI

The Coffin's Lullaby: Sleep Magick and Nightmares as Portals
Ashes of the Will: Rituals for Erasing the Self
The Fracture Rite: Shattering the Magickal Core
Funeral Candles: The Art of Emo Flame Magick
The Black Grimoire: A Blank Ritual for Writing in Absence
Phantom Thirst: A Halloween Survival Guide for Diabetes Insipidus
The Hollow Crown: Emo Royalty and Magick of the Outcast King
Sandpainting for the Soul
Falling Into Balance: Using the Extra Hour to Recalibrate Life
100 Southern Superstitions That Still Work
The DI Child: A Parent's Guide to Raising Hydrated, Happy Kids
The Jungle of Shame: Escaping the Hidden Lab of Doubt
The Witch's Toast: S'mores Spells and Creepy Confections
The Hoodoo Pantry: Spells from the Mason Jar
The Immortal Fortune: Secret Wealth Lessons from Captain Jack Harkness
The Specter's Embrace: Magick for Channeling Ghostly Lovers
Grateful Waters: A Thanksgiving Survival Guide for Diabetes Insipidus
The Seizure Gospel
Harvestbind: Autumn Sigils and Samhain Spells
Doctor Who: The Algorithmic Awakening
Silent Nights, Steady Waters: A Christmas Survival Guide for Diabetes Insipidus
The Extra Hour Effect: How One Hour Can Transform Everything
Blade Between the Breaths
Running with the Mountain Shadows
Echoes of the Failed Experiment – Becoming a Living Legacy

Swamp Witches & River Ghosts: Real Southern Hauntings

Cornbread Prophecies: Magical Recipes from a Southern Table

Doctor Who: The Signal in the Star

Bloomcraft: Spring Sigils and Equinox Enchantments

Vanisher: How to Disappear from the Internet Without Losing Your Life

The Ultimate Christmas Cookie Cookbook

The Unbreakable Parent: How to Mentally Survive Raising Kids in a Broken World

Time Debt: How to Reclaim the Hours You Didn't Know You Lost

One Month, One Million: Unconventional Cash Creation Tactics

Doctor Who: The Cyber Conversion Protocol

Black Friday Frenzy: The Art of Finding Hidden Online Deals

The Grimoire Buried Under the Apple Tree

Digital Couponing Masterclass: Your Step-by-Step Guide to Black Friday Savings

The Fire Inside the Flint

Shadows on the Ceiling: The Emo Guide to Astral Magick

The Bone-Eaters Beneath Us

Black Friday Bundle Blueprint: Creating Irresistible Product Packages for Maximum Sales

Thirteen Nights of Unbinding

Doctor Who: Engines of Influence

Pumpkin Spice Alchemy: Recipes of Fire and Frost

When Raptor Met Rexy: Prehistoric Lessons in Wild Romance

Oblivion's Candle: Burn the Path Behind You

Campfire Curses and Chocolate: A Halloween S'mores Grimoire

The Wallet That Wasn't Mine: Breaking Free from Inherited Scarcity
The Cola Zodiac: What Your Fizz Says About Your Fate
Frostfire Fortune: Unlocking Winter's Hidden Prosperity
Signal Jamming: Detox Your Brain from Info Overload
The Dust of the Forgotten Rite
The Golden Cat Sigils: Drawing Power in Bastet's Name
Mud Magick: The Prosperity of Getting Dirty
Savory Spicefall: Beyond the Pumpkin Pie
Pumpkin Spice Apothecary Kitchen
The Pumpkin Spice Economy: Turning Trends into Billions
The Ember Veil: 13 Nights of Fire Magick
Financial Freeze: When Earning Triggers Panic
The Gingerbread Alchemist: Sweet Recipes with a Twist
Biosynth Power: Programming Yourself from Scratch
Echoes from the Talking Circle
Truffle Alchemy: Fungus of Fortune
Spores of Power: The Truffle Witch's Handbook
Doctor Who: The Tower That Speaks
The Mycelium Veil: Truffle Magick Unbound
Broke But Ashamed: Healing the Shame Wound of Debt
The Evergreen Mind: Growth Through Winter Stillness
The Black Veil Truffle Rite
The Voice Beneath Symbols
Witchlight on the Bayou: Swamp Spells for Sovereignty
I Grew Up Poor and Now I Sabotage My Success
The Lantern of Hollow Souls
Shutdown Survival: A Citizen's Guide to Thriving When Government Stops
When Abundance Feels Like a Threat: Healing the Hidden Fears of Enough
The Scarecrow Grimoire
Owls of the October Veil

Candlewax and Curses: A Halloween Spellbook
Excavating the Inner Fossil – Transforming Fossilized Thoughtforms into Tools of Power
The Yule Witch's Spellbook: Magick for the Holiday Season
Haunted Christmas: Ghost Stories for Winter Nights
The Christmas Survival Guide: Thriving Through the Chaos
The Bone Orchard Rites
Haunted Commerce: The Ghost in the Marketplace
When Money Triggers the Inner Child
Silent Night with the Silence: A Christmas Thriller
The Lightning Crown: Living and Leading Through Seizures
TARDIS Tidings: Festive Stories from the Whoniverse
Autumn Reset: Slowing Down Without Falling Behind
The Trillion Dollar Soul: Rewriting the Currency of Reality
Truffle Eclipse Magick
Micro-Manifestations: Quick Magick That Works
5-Minute Rituals for Busy Witches
The Marshmallow Massacre: Halloween Treats with a Sinister Twist
Blood and Blackberry Thorns
Magickal Mornings: Rituals for a Blessed Christmas Day
Embers of the All-Hallows Fire
The Pumpkin Market Collapse
The Hour You Gained: Transforming Time Into Power
The Chamber Must Be Sealed: Mastering the Power of Controlled Access
The Cursed Manuscript of Petosiris
The Festive Hearth: Creating Holiday Traditions
Darkness Rising: Thriving as Nights Grow Longer
Harvesting Time: Turning the Year's End Into Your New Beginning
Petosiris and the 13th Zodiac Key
Wagewound: When Paychecks Become Identity Prisons

Walls That Watch

The Silent Feast: Rituals of Power in the Longest Night

The Distortus Legacy : Becoming a Deformed King in a Perfect World

The Hollow Masks

The Gratitude Furnace: Forging Gold from Thanks

Feast of Inner Gold: Eating for Energy and Enlightenment

Haunted Commerce: The Season of Spending Spirits

Fear Bonds: How Panic Creates Profit

Black Friday E-Commerce Playbook: Sales Tactics to Skyrocket Your Holiday Revenue

Budgeting for Black Friday: A Holiday Savings Planner

Haunting the Harvest Moon

The Warrior's Water: Emergency Preparedness for People With DI

The First Sip of the Year: A New Year's Survival Guide for Diabetes Insipidus

Doctor Who: The Thirteenth Node

The Unseen Struggle: Mental Health, Anxiety, and Chronic Thirst

The Hearth's Hidden Ledger: Counting Energies as Currency

The Gift Alchemist: Turning Any Offering Into Gold

The Papyrus of the Bound Spirit

The Magick of Leftovers: Transmutation in the Fridge

Frost and Fortune: Christmas Wealthcraft for the Modern Magus

Last-Minute Gifts: Creative Ideas on a Budget

10 Secrets to Surviving Holiday Crowds

The Witch's Dow Jones

The Witches' Graveyard Shift

Pumpkin Sigils: Carving Rites for Midnight Power

The Secret Shopper's Black Friday Guide: How to Get Early Access and VIP Deals

Fever in the Foundation
The Neuralyzer Reset: Reprogram Your Morning Routine
Lightning Lessons of the White Painted Woman
The Enchanted Snowflake
The Magic Sip: Surviving Disney Parks with Diabetes Insipidus
The One Who Draws Through You
Santa's Secrets: A Magical Holiday Planner
Silent Bells, Loud Miracles: Self-Help for the Season of Stillness
The Sugar Spell Codex: Confectionary Magick of Christmas
Autumn Hexcraft: Fallen Leaves, Fallen Barriers
Sleep Like a Fortress: Build a Life Where Insomnia Can't Survive
Nowhere Was Ever Home
Christmas Under the Stars: A Celestial Holiday Guide
Rentproof: How to Never Be Evicted Again
Workless: Escape the 9-5 Without Being Broke
The Gilded Gift: A Wealth Altar for Christmas Morning
The Black Friday Grimoire
The Hollowing: Ceremonies of Spiritual Collapse
Doctor Who: The Nameless Signal
Where the Eagle Hides His Courage
The Dwarf Tyrant's Ascent: Claiming Power in a World of Giants
The Currency of the Dead: Trading with Spectral Bankers
The Icebound Witch: Survival and Magick in the Cold
The Emergency Money Mind: Constant Crisis, Zero Calm
Thirst & Roses: A Valentine's Survival Guide for Diabetes Insipidus
Springing Into Clarity: Mastering the Energy Shift of Daylight Saving
Speed of the Nanotyrant: Agile Strategies for Life's Hunt

The 90-Day Reset: A Science-Backed Guide to Reinvent Yourself Before the New Year

The Coil of Thorns

Timegates Unleashed

Dopamine Fasting 2.0: Rewiring Your Brain in a World of Overstimulation

The Nanotyrannus Mutation: Embracing Your Differentiated Form

Unwritten January: How to Use the Blank Page of the Year to Re-Author Your Life

Feast of the Forgotten Spirits: Ancestor Magick for the Holidays

The Burnout Codex: A System for Thriving Beyond Stress

I Don't Deserve to Have Money

When the King Doesn't See You: The Shadow Predator's Guide

The Reset Ritual :A Guide to Shedding Last Year's Weight—Emotional and Physical—by Spring Cleaning Your Soul

Calendar Alchemy: Learn to Bend Time and Productivity around Your Natural Rhythms

The Mirror Contract: A One-Sentence Agreement with Yourself that Unlocks Real Change

The Nile Formula: Sacred Flow for Millionaire Minds

Forward Momentum: Productivity Rituals for the Lost Hour

Harvest Gold: Wealth Magick of Pumpkin Spice Commerce

The Magick of Christmas Lights: Illuminating Holiday Rituals

Cranberry Crown: Royal Self-Worth through Ritual Meals

Petosiris and the Worms of the Feathered Throne

The Evergreen Equation: Self-Help for Sustained Growth

The Rain Will Wash Us Away: Emo Weather Magick

Snowlight Shadows: Magick Under Frozen Stars

Doctor Who: Merger of Empires

The Bonewake Protocol

Extinction-Proof: How to Outlive Trends, Trauma, and Time

The Fourth Doctor: The Eccentric Wanderer

The Second Doctor: Chaos and Charm in the TARDIS (Patrick Troughton, 1966–1969)

The Third Doctor: Earthbound Defender of Time (Jon Pertwee, 1970–1974)

The First Doctor: Genesis of the Time Lord (William Hartnell, 1963–1966)

The Fourth Doctor: The Eccentric Wanderer *(Tom Baker, 1974–1981)*

The Fifth Doctor: Elegance and Empathy (Peter Davison, 1982–1984)

The Sixth Doctor: A Kaleidoscope of Conflict (Colin Baker, 1984–1986)

The Seventh Doctor: The Strategist of Shadows (Sylvester McCoy, 1987–1989)

The Eighth Doctor: A Time Lord's Renaissance (Paul McGann, 1996)

The War Doctor: A Time Lord's Burden (John Hurt, 2013)

The Ninth Doctor: The Healer of Worlds
(Christopher Eccleston, 2005)

The Tenth Doctor: The Lonely Hero (David Tennant, 2005–2010)

The Eleventh Doctor: The Madman in a Box (Matt Smith, 2010–2013)

The Twelfth Doctor: The Rebel with a Cause (Peter Capaldi, 2013–2017)

The Thirteenth Doctor: Breaking the Mold
(Jodie Whittaker, 2017–2022)

The Fourteenth Doctor: A New Beginning (David Tennant, 2022–2023)

The Fifteenth Doctor: Rewriting the Stars
(Ncuti Gatwa, 2023–2025)

Santa's Shortcut to Success: Micro Habits for a Better New Year

The Midnight Cocoa Manifesto: Comfort Rituals for Hard Nights

Why I Can't Save: Trauma Blocks to Financial Planning

Dino Brain, Mega Goals: Rewire Yourself for Savage Success.

Get Some Tarot cards: https://www.makeplayingcards.com/sell/apophis-occult-shop

Get some shirts: https://www.bonfire.com/store/apophis-shirt-emporium/

Instagrams:
@apophis_enterprises,
@apophisbookemporium,
@apophisscardshop
Twitter: @apophisenterpr1
Tiktok:@apophisenterprise
Youtube: @sg1fan23477
Hive: @sg1fan23477
CheeLee: @SG1fan23477

Podcast: Apophis Chat Zone: https://open.spotify.com/show/5zXbrCLEV2xzCp8ybrfHsk?si=fb4d4fdbdce44dec

Newsletter: https://apophiss-newsletter-27c897.beehiiv.com/

If you want to support me or see posts of other projects that I have come over to: **buymeacoffee.com/mpetchinskg**

I post there daily several times a day

Get your Dinowicca or Christmas themed digital products, especially Santa Raptor songs and other musics. Here: **https://sg1fan23477.gumroad.com**

Apophis Yuletide Digital has not only digital Christmas items, but it will have all things with Dinowicca as well as other Digital products.

www.ingramcontent.com/pod-product-compliance
Lightning Source LLC
LaVergne TN
LVHW022231200926
848481LV00006B/2225

* 9 7 9 8 3 3 0 6 3 1 6 3 6 *